Welcome to Beauty, Love, and Fear.

Come to these pages with your heart open. Come to them a stranger, come to them with gentleness, come to them with fondness, come to them deeply, and come to them with love.

Enjoy BLF.

1 Corinthians 16:14
"Let all that you do be done in love."

DEDICATION.
To you all.

I write and give this book to everyone who comes across its pages and to those who these words find. We share the world together, and you are a large part of the why of Beauty Love & Fear.

CONTENTS.

Part i.
Poetry & Stories

Intermission

Part ii.
Poetry and Stories continued.

Part i.

Beauty Love & Fear

Far beyond the reach of sight
there a place of beauty is, the air carries her tune to me.
I do not see a path but a leap of faith I must take,
So I Journey on, making my way.
The road is rocky, many things are unknown
but what else am I to do, other than to seek what is good?

On I press, through aching bones and bleeding flesh
in this adventure to fully be.
Whatever my plights may I know them whole
and whatever my fortunes may I share in them so.

I dare not cower to my burdens,
or discount my joys.
The way to, is through.
For beauty is the culmination of the adventure had,
from here to there.

Take me to the edge, should I dance into the unknown?
traversing the path of life,
am I gliding or crawling?
floating or falling?
Do I sit in my fear and watch my evil unfold?
or do I put on my best dress and dance till the sun goes to bed?
What am I to do?
God is that you?
Would you please give me your hand?

I came to be and as I came to be
I came carrying a fire within me.
Lit not by a match, but by an element beyond all stars.
It burns and burns, but it does not burn me,
it shows its light and power through me.
many things of Might seeking to quench,
but I hold this flame in a sheltering, never to meet the wind.

You are to me a tremble of sweet music,
my bones shudder at the touch of your fingers,
and my soul shivers with the love from your heart.

These lips each day remembers to whisper your name,
these eyes of mine study your face over every morning.
Who I to be without you, prefer not be that.
All my senses are given to the partaking in you.

I went about the world minding my own
when all of a sudden,
you were dropped into me, like anchor into sea.

And so appearing suddenly, as if to cause a beautiful chaos.
Like the meeting of the winds with the petals of spring, soft in its movement.
A reimagining of moments yet to be lived.
In beautiful chaos she came,
in daring beauty she lived,
and through cloudy and unclear eyes, was gone.
Life lived in a breath.

Inevitable a goodbye, as I say mine to you.
Cry if you have to, curse my death and be angry, but
know that your heart will sing again.
A beautiful melody.
A melody carrying the emerging spring, sweet enough
for sunlight breaking through the clouds,
for tweeting birds,
for blooming flowers.
For my darling, love will alway find you. How can it
not?

And I thought of the heart of me,
the heart of man.
How self seeking it is.
Adorned in "self love" but not a love for others.
how pretentious we are.
How pretentious you are.
How pretentious I am.
yet,
the motion of life remains,
the motion of life is to the other.
Therein, lies God.

I Sat With Myself Today.
I felt the grass under my feet, the green between my toes.
Birds singing, or crying, or laughing.
All the elements of sound unique to creation, inimitable.
Songs only they know, melodies only they make.
Fresh and new, this feeling of old.
I Sat With Myself Today.

I took to my imagination, the imagining of another,
I gave a face to the described,
a feeling to the written,
life to the imagined,
walls to a world.
From mind to pen, and pen to paper.

I Sat With Myself Today.

Why does the traveler travel?
To connect to the other, to nature, to find the extremes,
to experience difference, to marvel at God.
Why does the teacher teach and the preacher preach?
To and for the other.
The waiter, serves the other.
A leader, leads the other.
Why does one love another?
The measure to all these things may be for a living, an
earning, a connection, a yearning.
Life always without fail, connects to the other.
The manner in which we carry it out draws the
difference.

I Sat With Myself Today.

As she gets ready for bed,
and as she goes from yellow to golden,
pulling shut the blinds of day and ushering in the light of night,
as sweet music rings through to your soul, let it be understood that idle as we ought not to be, to be by yourself is not to be lonely.

I Sat With Myself Today.

I met a woman once.
Who was she?
I met a woman once. She was time, passing through me.
Caught in the corners of my eye, turning around, she was no more.
I met a woman once, only but for a singular moment, then gone.
I chased the wind, tirelessly, to the corners of the earth, empty.
I hope she was found.
With my soul heavy, my eyes closed, and my body weary,
I met a woman once, I think she never was.

I can't get to you,
but here's a photo of a flower I took for you.
I can't be with you,
but in my dreams, I create memories that remind me of you.
Hold me quick, don't let go.
But if you do, do it slow.

I looked up at the sky in the crow of night, there hung a crescent moon.
It told of a beauteous smile, the kind that adorns your face in the light of day, and under the moonlit night.

I am hung in your firmaments, and you in my orbit.
Forever pulling towards each other
here on earth and through all of Heaven.

I am weaved into the fabrics of your skin,
etched in the fine prints of the soul that you carry.
You are the red of my heart,
and the beating that it knows.

I dream dreams of beautiful places, but best of these, I dream dreams of you.

Holding on to the echoes of you in my dreaming,
you delight me as sky and ocean are gladdened by the colors of sunsets.
And just like sunset sees its end, so does a shared heart.
Left with fragments of what was, you walk on them as if on broken glass.

Gray is the world around
She brings with her a dull romance.
Falling to earth
exploding a billion different times.

Giving roses their scarlet,
cracking the sky and making her roar.
She makes me feel like a jazz ballad.
She leaves me her scent and sends me the sun.

For feelings, sad. For feeling lost, in the ticking of quiet limbo.

These words, I whispered to my shadow in the dark.

Are you there? If you are, please would you sing me to sleep?
All too familiar with the shadows, I fear bringing myself into the light.
But I have got to have a little bit of light, for with light shadows are created.
Maybe what I want is to hold on to the nothingness it shows me,
because then I will not have to face who I really am in full light.

I think I'm missing something, but I don't know what.
I think I lost something but I don't know where.
I am not entire, not without it.
It belongs in me, what is it?

Where do I go? How do I search?
How do I know where I am to look?

So many things are lost to us,
it's the ones who go seeking, who shall find.
So here is what I'll do,

I'll go searching for you, somewhere in the space,
between here and forever.

I paint the night with my dreams
because the world of the living is a hard scheme.
I am too much of a coward to fight for anything,
I'm a shell of a person.
I am empty.

But I do know, what it is to dream,
so perhaps I am more than it seems.
There may be hope for me yet,
there's a bit of fight in me left.

And as I emerge from the night, I'll emerge with these dreams,
to live them well, in this hard scheme.

Ruin held still.
Taking its time, seemingly inconsequential.
Silent in its consumption, unknowing to self.
Ruin, holds still.

If You Were Mine.

What a day it was. It was such a day most suited for love, as is everyday. Love had come down from heaven like it did every morning before humans woke up. To make it yet another day to bring two or more people together.
Love had the best job in the world, the most beautiful and poetic job. Love was most hated and most loved at the same time but Love never understood what it was to hate because all Love did was love.

Everyday Love would create friendships, reconciliations, kindness, patience, romances, and much more. Love indeed made the world go around.
Love, on this day, brought two people together. Marcus and Josephine. And as Love went about weaving their stories, they fell deeper for each other and then one day, Marcus asked Josephine if she would like to spend the rest of her life with him getting to know what and who Love really is. Josephine said yes, that she would really like to explore this matter for the rest of their lives. What a journey it would be.

They would very often express themselves and their promises to each other. And on one such day, by a river bed Marcus sat Josephine down and this is what he said:

"If you were mine,
I'll make another home for you in me. A place and person to whom you can be. A place and embrace, sturdy and warm.
I'll have the songbirds of dawn wake you up with a melody specially tuned for you. The sun will rise just to speak specifically of the light of your heart.
I'll sway the oceans to choreograph a dance of waves to illustrate your grand beauty. The flowers will come alive as they catch the scent of you when you walk by.
And when we feel the weight of this world, I will set sail across the grounds and seas of the earth to fetch you a bucket of laughter. I'll take your hand in mine, push your waist to mine, and we'll dance barefeet in the grass. Your voice, the music to our steps.
I shall call you mine and you shall call me yours.

I'll make winters feel as summers,
my shoulders and chest, as comfortable as pillows.
I want you to fall for me and I to you, to fall for me and I for you. Each waking morning, as new and constant as the daily miracle of the eyes catching first light.
I shall be your friend and your keeper. To your wounds I'll tend as we love even deeper.

I will always want to hold you,
I will always want to know you,
I'll tell you the burdens of my mind and I will listen for yours.
In our momentary dislike of the other, there still

wouldn't be another I would like more in the world.
And when things are tough, there isn't another place I'll
want to be but where you are.

I'll watch for the graying hairs and I'll love them.
I'll watch for the wrinkled skin and kiss them.
I'll watch for the slowing walk and I'll match them.
I'll watch our kids become our likeness , we'll marvel at
them.

If you were mine, here is some of what I'll do.
As best I can, I'll love you."

   Love sat at a distance, unseen, and listened. Love listened to the hearts of Marcus and Josephine as Marcus talked of his love for her. For Love could hear hearts as they spoke, although deceptive, Love could tell what truths were. As Love perhaps is the only one who knows what absolute truth is. So Love smiled and giggled at the joy of it all. He could hear the nerves and excitement in Marcus and could feel the reddening of Josephine's heart as Marcus spoke with poetic leaning.
Love, although being without hate and fear, knew that for humans and for life in this world many complications abound, and that they would face all manners of good and evil. Marcus meant every word he professed and Love could tell that both their hearts understood what it meant beyond the beauty of his expressions. Marcus would give himself to this love he had come to know through the very many emotions humans go through, and that Josephine would do the same.

Through their sufferings and through their joys, they would know completely in a manner, finite, what and who Love is. Because Love knew humans had limits here on earth, as Love is immeasurable, because Love is infinite.

Love got up, sighed a sigh of satisfaction. Then hearing a heart calling faintly for him, away in the far distance, gave one last listen to their hearts, bid them goodbye - although never leaving them as Love lives in the heart - and began the journey towards the call.
Who knows what becomes of Marcus and Josephine, we can only hope they let Love stay.
Forever.

I am known to you as you are known to me.
I hold no greater desire than to be given to you in totality and you to me in your entirety.

The days that most break my heart, I remember you in them.
I am no fool to the deceit of your heart nor the confusion of your tongue.
I heeded not the warnings of my head but gave play to the emotions of my heart.
A fool I can be, and what a foolish fool I was.

Turning my sadness into poems,
I refuse to drink you away.
Turning my pain into words,
beautiful hard things to say.

It's me, you, and this memory.
A future comes,
a moment had.
Time is spent,
and all is past.
It's just me now, and something resembling a memory.

Love & Loss

Man see woman, woman sees man
man's heart finds peace, her heart skips several beats.
He goes to her, she comes to him,
they become each others.

Down the aisle, a journey through life,
a happy home, some trying times.
Hands together, with each other,
a lot of cries, but more laughter.
Here comes a baby, then another.
What a family, happy together.

It's the middle of the night, she calls his name.
He wakes from his slumber, and kisses her face.
He feels the heat, she says it's a fever.
Down his spine, goes an unkind shiver.
Off to the doctor, a prayer is said,
he holds her hands, stays by her bed.

Weeks go by, boys miss their mom,
but daddy is around, and he stays strong.
Then comes a day,
daddy rushes away.

Children playing outside, car pulls up
It all feels wrong, so the playing stops.
Now all that is heard, are all the cries,
and then they knew, it was time to say goodbye.

On the day she is to go in the ground, these are some of the words he said in his heart;

"I'll smile for every memory of us, good or bad. I have enough for a lifetime. Maybe then, I won't have the space to feel the heartbreak of having you no more."

Time cut short, we've come to the end. This was a story about Love and Loss.

As breath holds life in dying,
let faith and hope hold heart and soul,
that man knows God and God be within man.
Guided like a light to shore,
certain like sun at dawn,
as peace covers you like moon slowly covers day,
let it be that breath holds life in dying.
Breathe! let life take over death as it lies in defeat.

And so this little one came to us,
in her mothers arms to cradle
in his fathers arms to be protected.
Out of me to love,
out of me to guide,
a joy to nurture and a pleasure to know.

You are this land to work,
a measure to toil for,
a garden to water and sweet fruit to bear.
She is an essence, one of joy, one of delight.
He is a presence, one of power, out of him, bold insight.

You are the honor of my life,
the warmth of your mothers heart.
I know no greater thing to be.

I bow before my father,
I kiss the cheeks of my mother.
I respect the toil of his hands, and the strength of his voice.
I adore the grace of my mother, and the home within her.

I do not rebuke her love, for I brought pain to her loins,
I run to his side when I feel the raging storms.
Her nights are given to me,
his rest i've taken from him.

I shake my fathers hand,
I take my mothers arm in mine.
I see the pride of a man when he looks in me,
I know the joy of a woman when she smiles at me.
I do not aim to make their hearts ache
A cheerful spirit within me they've made.

As I go along, I take them with me.
In heart and kind, my father and mother they'll always be.
I hug my father's chest
I embrace my mother's heart.

You remind me of rain,
that first trickle that grows into a familiar constant.
You remind me of pain,
the rolling of teardrops down the cheeks.
You remind me of snow,
beautiful and cold.
You remind me of the sun,
I adored your light but could never get close.

Remain still that I may make record of the glory of what you are.
That my eyes know the pulse, fleck, shimmer, and shine of yours.
That I know the soul you house through them,
that they receive me and be within me.

Remain still so I know every inch and bit of this moment.
How the air feels on my skin,
how the clouds move above us,
how your face traces the space in front of me,
how the ends of your lips shape.
Remain still next to me,
remain still here with me.

I got lost in the blues, the blues of your eyes.
You felt like beautiful colors that day. You still do.

It matters not how many times a thing I've done.
Doing them with you, makes it all new.

Whichever way I turn, I hear the call of adventure.
In the lands to the North,
in the peoples of the South,
the faraway longings of the East,
and into the waters of the West.

In Whatever direction I go, I feel the sway of adventure.
Looking up at the sky,
looking down in the depths,
and even when, I look into myself.

Intermission

A lot of things were drawn upon to bring you these words. One thing that struck me in particular was, as I wrote and crafted some of its pieces, in the writing of them I was making new discoveries in the instant, about myself and about life that I wasn't fully aware of or that presented themselves to me entirely fresh. There was a magic to those moments, it was sublime.

Beauty Love & Fear

Part ii.

Beauty Love & Fear

He was a stranger I met in a dining car on a train.
In between bites and sips, we talked about many things life and living.
In a moment of silence between thought and the watching of the night speeding by, without looking at me he said;

"I never learnt to finish things. I never met the ends of my beginnings. And when I am finished with this life, even in that death, I will have left my life incomplete."

I've met many strangers , they were for that moment.
I've had a number of friends, they were for a time.
I've had many experiences,
I've shared in and completed those moments.
All isn't meant for forever, and forever caters not to all.

My feet landed upon new ground,
It had its way of step,
but here upon entirely different terrain it had to start again.
To give its blood to the tasting of new rocks,
its flesh to the piercing of new thorns.
To learn new,
to harden its shell for this particular road.
For the journey of different paths, required different sacrifices.

Into one pit did everything go,
with one swirl did all things mix.
I knew not this from that,
everything became all
and all things became nothing,
formless and lost.

I lost reason,
gave over the reins to emotion.
I strangled life with the utterances from my tongue,
wielded hate and death upon them.
I lacked understanding
And most heartbreaking of these, I lacked love.

He came to me, for he needed a friend,
I scowled at him, broke his heart some more when it needed a mend.
I hid my smile and denied him my warmth,
back out into the cold I put him forth.
Into his dejection, he fell further,
a world littered with people, and he couldn't find a brother.
I love not my neighbor
And thus, love not myself.

I know not how to address the plight of my mind,
I know not how to dress the smile of my face,
eluding answers and truths,
How do you make your way out?
Is the question of this maze.

If this be my plight, may I meet it with nobility and grace, holding my chin up, my shoulders high and my chest out.

I wrestle with the path that calls for duty,
I struggle with the knowledge of my evil,
I fear it and need it.
How do I stop its fury?
How do I walk noble?

I got dealt a heavy heartbreak.
In that dealing I came to understand my heartbreak as such:
You, heartbreak, are a purging,
a scrubbing,
a necessary urging,
come to make way for a renewal of future loves coming.

I tried to run away from my life,
to seek it elsewhere.
Running from myself,
getting nowhere.
I tried to escape my shadow,
so I dimmed the lights.
I tried to escape the shallows,
because I had no depth inside.

Now here, where I am, is where all things are, it's where all things be.
There is naught ahead, there is naught behind.
Here where I am, that is where I wish to reside.

Actions they say, speak louder than words,
but do not discount words,
for they are a beckoning towards action.

Why should the mountain scare me?
It stands in mighty glory before me.
It may be menacing, yet it retains splendor.
It is mine to face, for it stands before my way.
With welling courage, it could teach me the lessons of
the climb, and at its peak, reveal a new world to me.

So wherever I come to and a mountain stands before
me,
may I understand her reason
may I summon my courage,
and may I scale her heights.

When my wings lacked strength of flight
You took your friend upon your shoulders
So he could feel the wind again
Till his wings grew stronger and he could trace his path
through the skies.

Come on!
Set fire to your hind,
spark the night, do not dim your days.
Run with the wind, weep with the rain.
Know stillness, make solitude a friend.
Trace the earth, see many souls.
That when it's all said and done,
You can love your end.

Oh you bones and flesh,
stiffen not thyself.
Move about the world, move with yourself.
Dance Dance Dance,
Let the blood flow.
Run Run Run,
that the ground your feet may know.
Play with the grass, climb up the trees,
fall into the water,
feel the wonderful breeze.
Oh bones and flesh,
get up on your feet,
trace this beautiful world
then fall on your knees.

Carry on weary bones
When your knees buckle and feet stumble,
Carry on weary bones
When your flesh bleeds and eyes weep,
Carry on weary bones
When you drop oceans deep and in you mighty fears creep,
Carry on weary bones
When time slows and what's ahead you do not know,
Carry on weary bones
You do not know what lies ahead but by God, you will fight your fears.
So carry on weary bones,
till victory comes or of your flesh, death becomes.

And when I am 80, and I sit in the fields,
that I see the world around
and love the life that I've lived.

I opened my eyes and across from me stood a familiar man,
I would come to call him father and he'll call me son,
together on the way we would go.
He sets me upon his shoulder and lifts me up to the sky,
he is teaching me to fly.
When doubt comes to me, he returns my gaze with reassuring eyes.
Whenever I fall, he's right there to steady me on.
Whenever I soar, with pride he cheers me on.
He teaches me much, he'll always be teaching me more.

Brother oh brother,
as pen to paper,
as tongue to speech,
as ears to music,
and as dance to feet.
So are you, to me.

Dear Love,
Dear Friend,
Dear Stranger,

Let me speak briefly on perfection.

If I am ever to expect it of you, or require it, mark me a hypocrite of intense measure and allow your legs carry you away from me as swiftly as they can conjure themselves. For I know not the reason and truth of forgiveness. I know nothing of life and Love.

Sincerely,
A Human.

Within grasp but out of reach,
I wanted you but my fingers couldn't quite find a thing to grip.
A blend of reality and mirage,
I don't see a way not to destroy something good in me, in the pursuit of you.

Once upon a time, a woman there was.
There was a tenderness to her face,
a tenderness to her walk,
a tenderness to her lips,
and a tenderness to the way she talked.

She cried around me once,
I was happy that it was in my arms.
Even that was tender.

If we had known more time,
perhaps we would have known more of each other.

Do you recognize me as I recognize you?
Instantly, becoming a dream I never did dream.
A dream I didn't know the need for till here before me
you were,
lacking not in clarity,
real as can be, you've become dreams' reality.

In the moments of time before, I knew not of your existence.
In a moment next, an existence without you seems not a life possible.
You begin life again,
and what's begun is rooted in the knowledge of you,
and so cannot have its moments without the fullness of you.

I would sooner let go of a bright star than let go of this love I have for you.
For God made many a stars but only one of you.

The depths of you, inexhaustible.
Your measure, from first moment runs through to the eternal.
You are in the dark of the cosmos,
and in the shine of the stars.
You extend to God and into the reach of the heart.
You are here with me, and you are through time.

You spark as sun wrapped by a constant lightning,
a beam of smiles as resounding as thunder enveloped in
beauteous clouds, pillowed against bluest sky.
You carry self in a manner draped by grace, a host of
angels look on and adore.
You're neither perfection nor purity but you are, I dare
say, the closest thing to full beauty in spirit and person
God has allowed me.

That world inside your head, rest it on my shoulders.
That Well inside of your eyes, empty it on my chest.

Whisper into my ear the many music of you,
set this sight of mine upon the many glories of you.
Give me the many feels of your seasons,
share with me Gods many reasons.
Dancing about in the air of you
flow to me from the massive wells of you.
Oh from the art of you,
comes the bountiful joys of you.

Sparkle,
a rain of tiny diamonds falling through the shine of burning sun.

Illuminate,
a beaming of star power as if out the majesty of Angel presence.

Iridescent,
a giving of me in collective beauty as shown by a rainbowed sky.

Glow,
a continuous insistence on emission of the light of life.

I sat amongst the winds,
I shared the air with the leaves atop the tallest trees.
She did her dance and rang through me,
like the singing of wind chimes, she rang in me.
I sat amongst the winds,
she swayed me forth and brought about goosebumps and chills.
She leapt across the surface, then wrapped herself around me.
She did this beautifully, I might add,
then danced away.
I sat amongst the winds today.

I want for night, to turn to day.
I want for My Love, to come and stay.
I Want for life, to live and play.
I Want for these things, to have and hold, today.

The wounds upon and in me stand to be a mark proving that I did live. Be it scars from a bicycle fall, or tears from an old love.

If time sang a song, what would it be?
A ballad of joys,
an expression of sorrows,
a tale of heroes
or a song of terrors?
Would the winds aid her in her tune?
The waters bare themselves as tears?
Would mountains stomp and sway?
Would life speak of its best, or its fears?
If time sang a song, what would that song be?

Every joyful hello of life does become a heartbreaking goodbye.

I'm glad you shared your time with Beauty, Love and Fear.
Much Love.

Beauty Love & Fear

AFTERWORD

The journey of BLF started when I began to write more intently when I lived in Lexington Kentucky. At the time, these pieces did not know they'd be making their appearance in a book.
The idea for BLF was born at the beginning of 2024, although the desire to write a book has always accompanied me. As it came, it did so with the flow of many more of its pieces which have mostly been included in the compilation that makes up this book.
It takes a village, and as we all need each other to make our way through life, here are a few people from my village to whom I owe a massive thank you in the journey of BLF.

My younger brother King.
As my most constant companion through our lives together, there isn't much to my life without your presence in it. And God knew that. Having your support, encouragement and presence has been most wonderful in my desire to be better. Thank you.

My Father, Hemen Gar.
I would need to write another book to fully encapsulate what you mean to me. A big part of BLF is inspired by you, your romance with our mother, and how much I look up to you. Your wisdom amazes me everyday, and because of you I am excited to be a father someday. Thank you.

Kemi.
You have shared your time and have been a bouncing board and a test run for some of these words from their infancy to their sure positions on these pages. I can't express enough, how much of a good friend you have been to me and to BLF. Thank you.

Damola
You have always sought to move me along in my ventures, to elevate my life, and prop me up. Thank you.

Aunty Doom
Nobody champions me as fervently as you do. You give yourself to us generously. Thank you, for reading some of these words and for encouraging me in my writing.

To my Loosier Family (Steven, Amanda, Camryn and Sophia), what a blessing you are to me and King. You're always standing by our side. Mrs Amanda, thank you for enjoying the parts of BLF you first saw and loving its words. Thank you.

To Mrs Hudspeth for our conversations, to Pastor & Author Shane Yancey, for your advice and guidance in going about publishing. To both the unseen and expressed support of family, friends and acquaintances alike. Thank you all, immensely. Share Beauty Love and Fear with each other. Until next time, your friend.

Beauty Love & Fear

Title and name design by Oluwakemi Akande.
Front and back cover design and photograph, by Dondo H. Gar.

Beauty Love & Fear

Beauty Love & Fear

Milton Keynes UK
Ingram Content Group UK Ltd.
UKHW042141281024
450365UK00001B/23